Make Your Own Paper Cuts

Animals of the Chinese Zodiac

by Xu Dengxiang

Better Link Press

On the Cover
The Goat
This paper cut is marked by its neat and crisp style. A magpie by a cloud, which through its stylization can be recognized as an "auspicious" cloud, congratulates the sheep with good news. This represents luck and good fortune in the "Year of the Goat."

Top
Chrysanthemum
In this work the chrysanthemum seems to be swaying in the wind, making the work dynamic. The lines of the chrysanthemum are succinct, abstract and very modern.

This book is edited and designed by the Editorial Committee of *Cultural China* series

Paper Cutting Works by Xu Dengxiang
Text by Community Center of Youyi Road in Baoshan District, Shanghai
Translation by Cao Jianxin
Photographs by Gong Gandi
Design by Xue Wenqing

Copy Editor: Kirstin Mattson
Editor: Yang Xiaohe
Editorial Director: Zhang Yicong

Senior Consultants: Sun Yong, Wu Ying, Yang Xinci
Managing Director and Publisher: Wang Youbu

ISBN: 978-1-60220-151-4

Address any comments about *Make Your Own Paper Cuts: Animals of the Chinese Zodiac* to:
Better Link Press
99 Park Ave
New York, NY 10016
USA

or

Shanghai Press and Publishing Development Company
F 7 Donghu Road, Shanghai, China (200031)
Email: comments_betterlinkpress@hotmail.com

Printed in China by Shanghai Donnelley Printing Co., Ltd.
1 3 5 7 9 10 8 6 4 2

Contents

The Art of Chinese Paper Cutting

Paper cutting is one of the oldest and most widespread of the traditional decorative arts in China. It is marked by simplicity, directness, brightness and a sense of antiquity. In 2009 this important art form was inscribed in UNESCO's representative list of the "intangible cultural heritage" and recognized as being in need of protection.

To create paper cuts, only a few inexpensive materials are needed. Practicing this art can not only improve the hands' flexibility and coordination, but also develop one's sense of patience and creativity. Paper cutting is an ideal leisure activity, helping to ease the stress and strain of life today.

Artistic Principles

A work of paper cutting should be characterized by a simple and bright image, a tidy and abbreviated form, defined lines and aesthetic appeal.

First of all a paper cut should have a defined theme before any cuts are made. Chinese paper cutting mainly adopts the technique of "scattered dots in perspective," which means it represents a flat picture, without three-dimensional perspective. It also does not use any shading, i.e. transitioning from light to the dark. With their bold images and appealing themes, paper cuts are extremely accessible and eye-catching.

In terms of form, Chinese paper cutting is marked by exaggeration and distortion. The most characteristic parts of human figures, plants or animals should be featured by giving them special prominence or enlarging them. A true work of paper cutting art requires repeated consideration and study.

Youyi Folk Paper Cutting

This books focuses on paper cutting techniques popularized in the Youyi area, Baoshan, which

Early Morning Melody
This paper cut is characterized by its perspective, which is unusual in showing a scene from above. In early morning a flock of small birds fly over the local residences with white walls and red tiles. This scene looks like music notes on a staff singing an early morning melody of daily life. Based on an original engraving by Wen Yumei.

lies north of Shanghai. This area is one of the traditional centers of folk paper cutting, and in recent years a group of artists, headed by Xu Dengxiang, has explored new techniques. For example they have experimented with creating paper cuts by combining knife cutting and adhesion. In addition, by drawing on such artistic forms as engraving, they have gradually evolved in style from traditional paper cutting to a modern expression of the art. Paper cutting of this kind is marked by its decorative style featuring meticulousness and exaggeration, with extremely obvious features.

In order to further popularize this folk art, and the culture that has produced it, the neighborhood community center of Youyi Road in Baoshan has, since 1989, offered courses on paper cutting. They have promoted the art

The Lotus Flower
A group of small fish swims joyfully in the water. Following each other head to tail, the fish have at their center the lotus flower, lotus pods and lotus leaves. The composition features a circle inside a square, giving prominence to the beautiful and graceful lotus flower in full blossom. Based on an original engraving by Shi Yun'e.

form at centers of cultural activities in different residential areas, schools and communities, as well as setting up paper cutting saloons. The group has also compiled instructional books such as *Introduction to Folk Paper Cutting Art* in China, and provided practical guidance for more and more students. Their students have attended contests at various levels, with many emerging as award winners.

Techniques

There are mainly two kinds of paper cutting: symmetric (using folded paper) and plane (on unfolded paper). Typically the outer outline is cut before the patterns inside the work, moving from the outside in.

In symmetric paper cutting a piece of paper is folded before a piece of complete work is brought about through cutting. This is the form most commonly seen in Chinese paper cutting.

Compared by symmetric paper cutting, plane paper cutting is freer, hence requiring a higher level of technique. The cutting is usually undertaken directly after the conception of the work.

Joyful Magpies on a Plum Tree
This work, which draws on the traditional folk pattern of "clustered flowers," features meticulous and fine lines. The design of well balanced plum blossoms and magpies results in a warm and joyous atmosphere.

Materials and Tools

Scissors are the most important tools for paper cutting. They should be chosen to suit the size of the hands of the maker, making sure that they feel comfortable to use. They should also have the appropriate tightness and sharp blades as well as sharp, regular tips. For children it is safer to choose scissors with blunt tips.

Paper is the basic material used for paper cutting. Usually, relatively thin, flexible and durable paper is chosen. There will be breaks if the paper is hard and crisp, leading to the inability to create detailed work and a decrease in artistic effect. The color can be chosen according to the purpose and theme. Generally speaking, red is chosen for the celebration of traditional festivals. Paper cuts in white, black and blue, which have a strong modern appeal, are popular among young people.

Waves of Wheat
In this image, small birds fly across wheat fields. The representation of abundance and the warm golden tint express the joy of harvest. Based on an original engraving by Zhang Zhiming.

Paper Cuts of the Twelve Animals of the Zodiac

In ancient China people adopted twelve different animals to symbolize time through their characteristic activities and features. Each animal represented a period of time in a day; in ancient China a day was divided into twelve periods of two hours each. They also came to represent the progression of years, and today we call certain years, the "Year of the Tiger" or "Year of the Goat," etc.

The order of the twelve animals is as follows: mouse (or rat), ox, tiger, rabbit, dragon, snake, horse, goat, monkey, rooster, dog and pig.

Since ancient times people have lived in close relationship with animals. For many centuries human description and depiction of animals have reached a very high artistic level. Many paper cutting enthusiasts find that these twelve animals provide an interesting and effective way to delve into the practice of the art form.

In this book you can discover your personal zodiac animal and create a beautiful paper cut of your own!

Do It Yourself

Rat

This industrious and agile animal is able to dig holes, climb trees and hills, and cross rivers. Its long tail serves to balance the composition of the paper cut, so attention should be given to the tail's features. The arc of its legs should be round and sleek, and its eyes spirited.

Ox

An indispensable partner to farmers in traditional China, this animal is often seen in paper cutting. Its bold horns and large eye are two important features.

Tiger

It is marked by strong leg muscles, short front legs and longer rear legs, as well as long and powerful claws. Cutting should start from the claws, with particular attention paid to the artistic effect of the stripes on its back. Its tail should curve naturally.

Rabbit

An example of the exaggeration typical in paper cutting, its ears are longer than those of a real rabbit. Its tail is short and clustered, and the curved outline conveys a sense of motion. The arc of its eyes should look natural rather than protruding.

Dragon

The only imaginary animal among the zodiac animals, it signifies power, nobility and dignity. Its body looks like that of a snake. Its sense of towering scale and dynamic momentum can only be brought about through a curved outline.

Snake

Appearing long and cylinder-shaped, its extended body is presented in a coiled format in paper cuttings. The spirit of a snake is also invoked through its raised tail and forked tongue.

Horse

The horse has played an important role in human life for thousands of years. In paper cutting, its mane and tail should be undertaken with a focus on decorativeness, combining realism with aesthetic appeal. Its four limbs should look strong and powerful.

Goat

This animal is thought of as gentle, elegant and sentimental. Its figure is marked by short and robust limbs, a wide and flat back, and a round, thick body. Its beard is another major distinguishing feature. Only meticulous and sensitive cutting can capture its representative characteristics.

Monkey

This animal is known for its great flexibility and agility. In traditional Chinese culture, an image of a monkey is often combined with a peach, which stands for longevity. When cutting, attention should be paid to the area between the monkey and the peach, and due prominence given to the peach.

Rooster

The rooster was described by ancient people as an animal of courage and benevolence as well as trustworthiness. Since in Chinese its name sounds like the word for "auspicious" it is a symbol of luck and good fortune. Prominence can be given to its beautiful and proud tail-feathers.

Dog

This bright and wise animal is known for its loyalty. In the course of cutting, attention should be paid to its raised head and curved tail. In addition the patterns added to its body increase its aesthetic appeal.

Pig

The pig is a clever animal, standing for wealth and leisure in traditional Chinese culture. The tail in the paper cut should be tiny and cute, and the image will be more vivid if there are cuts made to create a wrinkled nose.